T0209028

Cried
MYSELF TO
Life

Cried
MYSELF TO
Life

CAROL DAYS

WESTBOW
PRESS*
A DIVISION OF THOMAS NELSON
& ZONDERVAN

WestBow Press books may be ordered through booksellers or by contacting:

WestBow Press
A Division of Thomas Nelson & Zondervan
1663 Liberty Drive
Bloomington, IN 47403
www.westbowpress.com
1 (866) 928-1240

ISBN: 978-1-5127-1115-8 (sc)
ISBN: 978-1-5127-1116-5 (e)

Library of Congress Control Number: 2015914577

Print information available on the last page.

WestBow Press rev. date: 9/15/2015

In memory of my husband, Elder Anthony Days Jr., a man with a heart for God and people, a warrior on the streets and in the prisons, a wonderful father, and a true friend to many.

He left behind a legacy of unwavering faith, commitment, and dedication to preaching the Word of God. As a husband, there were thirty-three years of love, friendship, and devotion like no other—and laughter to last a lifetime.

To my girls, who fill my life with joy every day. Your shoulders have been a source of strength, love, and comfort to me daily. Thank you for giving me the support and encouragement I needed to follow my dreams. You are my warriors.

To my grandson, who has elevated me to a higher level of love, and to the person who holds the umbrella for me when it rains—one glance at the door, and there you were.

Contents

Acknowledgments xi

Introduction xiii

Chapter 1   Life 1

Chapter 2   Death 3

Chapter 3   Grief 5

Chapter 4   Friends 7

Chapter 5   Faith 9

Chapter 6   Wisdom 12

Chapter 7   Prayer 15

Chapter 8   Fear 17

Chapter 9   Finding Your Purpose 20

Chapter 10   Friendship 22

Chapter 11   Solitude 24

Chapter 12   Invest in Someone's Future 26

Chapter 13   Embrace the New You 28

Chapter 14   Love 30

Chapter 15	Do You Choose Dreams or Love?	32
Chapter 16	Real Love	34
Chapter 17	Pause	36
Chapter 18	Living Life as a Joy and Not a Chore	38
Chapter 19	Second Chance	42
Chapter 20	Being Different	46
Chapter 21	Foundation	48
Chapter 22	Suddenly	51
Chapter 23	Nuggets for Life	53
Chapter 24	Finally	55

Acknowledgments

I thank God for allowing me to write this book. From the very beginning, it was just between the two of us. Whenever doubt or fear came, God gave me peace of mind to continue. I am learning a lot in my walk with God. Each day is filled with adventure and great expectation, and for this I say thank you.

Introduction

Of everything in the world, life is the one thing for which we should be most grateful, yet it's the one thing most taken for granted. If only we could understand the hope and love God had when he planned us, we would see how truly precious we are to him and the hope he has for us to live a good life. Though some look upon this gift of life with little or no regard whatsoever, it's only when we feel the true essence of God's love that we are filled with the desire to carry love and compassion in our hearts for one another. Living is God's ultimate gift to each of us. What we do with our lives is our gifts back to him.

1

Life

Life—what can I say? It truly is what we make it. All of our hopes and dreams are before us every day. Do we stop to think about how we wish our lives away? I wish I had this; I wish I lived there; I wish I looked like that; I wish I could be like that. If only we could channel that energy into being thankful for who we are and what we have, we would see how truly amazing our lives already are. We get so consumed with society and how we are viewed by others that we miss the basic fundamentals of life—and that's living it. We all have the ability to change our lives for the better, each and every day. It's how we choose to use our time and energy that makes us who we are. By learning to focus on ourselves, being true to ourselves, and being the very best that we can be, we will discover how truly unique and special we are.

I have found life is like a roller coaster—full of highs and lows. Each day is full of decisions that help shape my destiny. When I wake up and thank God for allowing me to see another day, I lay the foundation for a good day—a day full of hopes, dreams, and possibilities.

It costs nothing to say thank you—a small act of gratitude to God for all he has done in our lives. And God, being who he is, loves us regardless. When I think of the goodness of Jesus and all he has done for me, how can I *not* say thank you? He is a God of love and of second, third, and fourth chances.

Each day is another opportunity for me to get my life right, and I thank him every day for that. I thank him for grace, mercy, and forgiveness, which only he can give to me—what a combination. With these three things alone, I have a recipe for success. I am learning to let my own individual light shine.

If we knew how important we are and how precious we are in the sight of God, we would have no time for wishes but only praise, worship, and a grateful heart as we strive to go throughout our day.

2

Death

When my husband died, it was the moment in my life when the world stood still. I was afraid to move or to speak, and I could not hear anyone's words. I was in a space where everything was spinning faster than sound. I could find no peace anywhere. Everything was out of control, whirling around so fast until I had nothing left in me. Lost and confused, I went about each day, searching for some form of understanding. Then, finally too exhausted to do anything else, I found a nice, comfortable shell in which to rest—a dark and quiet place, where nothing else could reach me; where there was no room for spinning around; where I could sit and not think about anything or anyone. By doing this, I gave myself permission to have the ultimate pity party.

This went on for several days, and I truly lost track of time.

I later realized this was a part of the healing process that I needed. I wanted to pray but couldn't. I needed to sleep but couldn't. I needed to eat but couldn't. Things were truly out of my control. I was angry at my situation. I felt cheated. I felt robbed of my future. I was thrown out of my safe comfort zone, years in the building. But life continued, despite what I was going through and regardless of my circumstances.

Then, after several days of looking and feeling my worst, a crack appeared in my shell. It was a small crack but large enough for light to creep through it. With the light came fresh air and sunshine, followed by a sense of clarity. I looked at myself and realized I had people in my life who depended on me. I was Mom. At this point I remembered I had a purpose.

I also discovered I had the most amazing daughters in my world. They were my warriors, and they did what warriors do— take charge. I have never been more amazed to see these young women go into action. Their dad would have been as proud of them as I was. It was family, coming together.

My shell finally fell off after a few weeks, and there I was, through it all and still standing. At that moment when I felt my weakest, I was strong beyond words. God's Word settled in my heart, and I began to overcome my feelings of despair and misery. By taking my walk of faith each day, I began a new life journey. As unprepared for it as I was, each day got better. Life goes on.

3

Grief

G rief is one of life's most painful experiences. If you have ever been there, you know. My, how unprepared I was for this big, fat emotion. Believe me when I say that it will knock you completely off your feet. It will knock the wind out of you and have you coasting downward on that roller coaster of life.

But grief has to run its course. There is no way around it. God, I hated it—don't we all?—but this too is included in the circle of life. I personally hated the feeling of loneliness, of knowing my life as I knew it would never be the same. It amazed me how, in seconds, my life changed. What in the world was I going to do? How could I grieve and think at the same time? This was more than I was prepared to handle.

I began to lose sight of reality, and fear started creeping in. The unknown is called that for a reason. I was not a quitter—that wasn't an option—so I realized I had to talk to God to make it through this time in my life. My head was so full of emotions—sadness, hurt, fear, and a feeling of complete turmoil—I was afraid to blink.

So I began to pray to God. I prayed and talked, and I talked and prayed for months, trying to understand the unexplainable. By staying focused on God and not on my situation, I knew he would bring me through this time in my life. Days and weeks slowly went by. Then, gradually, my life began to come into focus, like a picture being developed.

I'd gone from being two to one. I'd gone from being "she who must be pleased," as my husband had called me, to "if I don't do it, it won't get done." At this point, my flesh said, "Life stinks!" But what a perfect opportunity for God to remind me that I was still here. I could think, walk, and talk, and, believe it or not, I was still in my right mind. Do you realize how often we take that for granted?

It was during this season of my life that I became Humpty Dumpty. When I fell, small pieces of my life spilled all over the place. I cried and I cried—until I cried myself back to life. I told God I didn't know what to do, what to think, or how to feel. I needed him. What a feeling of comfort in knowing I was not alone. Even though I had to find my way through this grief, it was not bigger than God.

I had to figure things out for myself. Others were depending on me. Any decisions I made affected not only my life but others as well. Talk about putting the cap back on the bottle. There was no time to fake it until I made it. Life was moving like a train, and I had to get a seat.

4

Friends

I have the most wonderful friends in the world. I would not have made it without them.

Friends may come and go. Some are seasonal, passing through your life. Others are like a branch sprouting from your heart. They have permanent residence. There is nothing in life better than a true friend—someone to laugh with when you have those "what was I thinking?" moments; someone who will walk beside you in a storm and not be afraid to get her hair wet.

A true friend will look at you in the middle of your worst day and still stand by your side. When you say something you shouldn't say, a true friend forgives you because he knows your true heart. She will warn you if you are heading in the wrong direction and be there with open arms when you return. He will not judge you, because that's not in the true-friend handbook.

You never have to impress a true friend because she always sees only you. You not only share the same essence but the same heart.

I thank God for my friends—and you know who you are.

5

Faith

We have all heard that faith is believing something without actually seeing it. This is difficult for some of us because we are a visual people. Everything is so in our faces that if we don't see something, we don't have time for it.

My true test of faith was in believing God's Word despite what was happening around me. Waiting, trusting, and believing while in the midst of a storm is not an easy thing to do. Regardless of what happens, your life has a way of going forward anyway.

Knowing that faith is the driving force in any situation has helped me. I know I can ask God for anything, and nothings too big or too small for God. God loves to be put to a test. Our problem is often that we ask for small things. I finally realized there is no limit to what God can do. My whole mind-set changed when I found myself in a situation and realized there was no other way out than to ask God for help.

God will show up and show out in your life, if you let him. Specific thoughts and desires in our hearts are the things with which he wants to bless us. All we have to do is ask. That simple act of faith can change our lives forever. A home, car, job, and relationships are there for the asking, and God wants us to ask for them.

You know those secret prayers that only you and God know? I get excited when I think about mine, because I tell God that my life, dreams, hopes, and desires are all in his hands. Believe me—I can do "stupid" pretty good on my own. I want to be able to make sound decisions in my life. For that, I don't look to anyone to direct my steps but God.

I tell my kids that God and I are tight—"Like that," I say as I cross my fingers. That is my level of faith. God has blown my mind and had me nearly speechless—all I could say was "Who woulda thunk it?" What a mighty God we serve. Dare to test your faith by sharing with others the amazing goodness of God in your life.

As I've continued to grow and seek him, I've discovered there are so many ways to lift up Jesus. Witnessing, sharing, educating, caring—all of these are ways to help change someone's life. Everyone is not called to be a preacher, but everyone is called to tell of the goodness of God. When you realize what you are made of—the DNA of God—nothing should keep you from walking and talking in victory.

I ask God every day for a miracle. Being human, I often expect to see something larger than life happen to me. Then it dawns on me that just because I didn't get my larger-than-life miracle doesn't mean it didn't happen. Maybe I was someone's miracle, just by speaking, smiling, or asking about a person's day. The things of God are free and easy. You will be amazed at what you are capable of doing in your life and the lives of others.

With life, remember to "keep it moving." This was something my husband said constantly. I believe you should not look back on your life journey with regrets. It's impossible to go forward otherwise. Memories are designed to be carried in your heart, a place where they can be thought of with joy, laughter, and love—it's where lessons can be learned, where wisdom takes root and grows.

Don't get stuck in a place you were supposed to pass through in life. Stop looking through tinted windows. Your circumstances do not dictate your worth. You may wash dishes today and own the same restaurant tomorrow. You may be uncomfortable speaking to a crowd but can write coherent words on paper. Stop dreaming, and start living—life is too short.

Dare to make a difference in yourself. Don't be afraid to participate in your own life. Discover the writer, director, and producer in you. You have the ability to change your situation for the better. If you were unhappy with today, tomorrow is your opportunity to make your life better. All you have to do is trust and believe that there are greater things waiting for you.

And learn to pray from your heart. Don't give the Devil any space for editing in your life. Trust and believe in uncommon favor. It's there for the asking.

6

Wisdom

Another ingredient in life is wisdom. When you ask God for this, watch out! Wisdom changes everything from black-and-white to color—I mean, the high-definition color that shows everything. This brings new meaning to the phrase, "What happens in the dark comes to light." That's because there is no darkness, only light.

Scary, right? Wisdom is knowing that you don't need to run when you can walk—you will still get where you are going. The difference is that by running, you will miss details. So often, we take very simple things in life for granted—the very essence of things (sound, color, taste, smell) and details that are essential to life.

Wisdom is knowing when to stand for something and when to walk away. Things are not always as they seem; wisdom tells you this. I have learned to seek understanding when I have doubts and not always make assumptions. The Bible is there for clarification. I'm not afraid to ask questions, and I try to keep an open mind.

Wisdom is allowing God to minister to me daily. Seeking knowledge is very important; growth comes from knowledge. I am learning not to miss the details of my life by moving too fast. I am slowing down and embracing the details because I know there are moments in life I will never get back.

This was where I prayed for clarity in my life. I was searching for that perfect fit for me. We all have talents and gifts. Some of us will be fortunate enough to discover, enjoy, and share our talents with the world. Others of us will search for a lifetime. That's why it was important for me to get to know myself.

I was a wife and mom. For years, this was my world, and what a beautiful place it was—a place designed to last me a lifetime; my comfort for life. Suddenly, life happened, and there I was—broken into. I will always be a mom, but there is also me. Getting to know "me" has been very exciting. I take small steps as I navigate through my new life. I pray for wisdom to avoid unnecessary setbacks and pitfalls in my daily life.

Wisdom lets me know that I don't know everything, and that's fine. I have learned to listen more and appreciate each day as it comes. Silence can be golden.

Then I had to realize that every battle is not mine. Every problem is not mine to solve. I am responsible for things that happen in my life. It takes all my strength to stay focused on me. When I am led to help someone, then through prayer and obedience, God's will shall be done in that person's life.

I don't have to be in the midst of every situation that happens around me. I have found great satisfaction from cheering someone on from the sidelines. I always wanted to be a cheerleader!

7

Prayer

My advice is to never leave home without prayer—it's
your very own secret weapon. The more you use it, the
stronger and more powerful you will become. Praying during
a storm is easy; it's the most natural thing to do. Learning to
pray before the storm and being thankful after the storm is
something else.

I pray and thank God for every detail in my life—for waking
me up; for my life, health, strength, sound mind, and family.
Prayer is so powerful. The line of communication with God is
what life is all about. No one wakes up every morning feeling
spiritual. I have to pray for wisdom, just to pray to get my day
started. By praying to God and asking for help, I can rewrite or
edit changes in my life.

Just because I woke up in a storm doesn't mean it will rain

all day. I also pray for those who don't know how to pray for themselves. It's an action of faith, followed by a reaction by God. The more I trusted God with my life, the more I began to see changes unfold. I had to get ready, because life waits for no one.

Prayer is being smart enough to realize you cannot handle every situation on your own. Listening to instructions is not only easy, but it also paves the way for changes in your life. The most natural thing to do in a crisis is to pray. What we have to do is receive our blessings regardless of whether it's the answer we wanted, because our lives are not our own.

Only by putting on my cape and going through the ups and downs of life did I find unusual power—power to navigate the storms of life. The sun may not be shining outside, but it can shine in your heart.

Living is the best reason to be happy; let your light shine. A word of caution: have your sunglasses handy when you see me coming.

8

Fear

Fear can put the brakes on your life quicker than anything. It's so easy to say, "Don't be afraid. You can do it. Don't be afraid of change in your life." Change is something that usually happens gradually. You can prepare for it. You have an opinion on whether change is even necessary in your life.

Unexpected change is something else entirely. Unexpected change caused me to step out of my comfort zone—and it was not a good feeling. It brought stress at all levels, and my mind went in circles, searching for peace and direction. I found that it's okay to feel uncomfortable in life—that's where I found my inner strength.

You will never know what you can do until you start doing something. Life is like a road. You have intersections and corners. If you get lost at an intersection, take it as an opportunity to make a decision. If you make a wrong turn in life, you don't have to keep going in that direction. That's what U-turns are for. Turn around at that point, and keep turning until you are back on track. You may need a GPS when you drive on the roads but not for life; in life, you need only God.

When I conquered certain levels of fear in my life, I changed from being Mickey Mouse to being one of the Avengers. I had all kinds of power just waiting to be activated.

I can encourage someone. I can guide someone through his darkest hour. I can stand in prayer for someone. I can say that one thing that someone has waited a lifetime to hear. I can tell someone about Jesus.

Stand boldly on God's Word, and say, "Don't you see this cape blowing behind my back?" It's an original cape, made just for me and full of power and love. It was purchased with a price, and it's nonrefundable. It's the cape of life. Don't leave home without it.

There are two important keys to life: (1) knowing who you are, and (2) being true to who you are. When I think of some of the really dumb things I have done in my life. I tell God I'm sorry so quickly—and God knows I really mean it. My dad always told me that "fear of the Lord is the beginning of wisdom." Don't fear advice, instruction, or rebukes in life. These things only make you stronger and wiser. Life is like a school with no breaks. The more we learn, the more we realize there is so much more in life to learn. Keep an open mind, and "keep it moving."

Don't be afraid to live. Don't let fear dictate your every move. Opening my heart to change was the smartest thing I ever did. The opportunities I found were limitless. Hopes and dreams were overflowing. What I felt was the end was only the beginning. The sun began to shine through the clouds. Making a decision regarding my life was not hard. Moving forward was not hard. And living by faith helps me continue, day by day.

9

Finding Your Purpose

I had to find my purpose. I had to find out who I was. The road I chose would make all the difference in my life. Once I was on the right path, then there was no turning back. What was that one thing I enjoyed doing more than anything? What was that one thing I saw myself being good at?

God has empowered each of us with greatness. You can either wear your greatness on a T- shirt for the world to see, or trust God to help you be the best person you can be. I had hopes and dreams for myself. I felt some were obtainable but others not so much. That's the good thing about life. As long as you live, you can dream. So my everyday miracle is knowing there is nothing too hard for God.

I made a decision to change my way of thinking. I wanted to stir up the gifts in me. I knew if I just trusted in God, there was no telling how bright or far my light would shine. People will say, "I didn't know you could do that," but God knew. I have heard it preached over and over again that if you don't use your gift, God will give it to someone else. So I decided to pray for guidance—whatever gift I had, I wanted it to be manifested. I wanted to be a blessing to someone. I wanted to make God smile. The one thing I knew more than anything was myself. Here again, I had to be careful what I prayed for. I wanted what God had for me. I didn't want to create a talent and run with it. I wanted to stay in his will.

I knew the Word and the part it played in my life. There were things I could share to help someone. I didn't like the spotlight; I didn't thrive on attention. I was not comfortable with speaking in front of people.

But I trusted in God. He has a way of letting his will for our lives shine through our fears. I found a place of comfort—a place where I can encourage someone. It's exciting and natural, and nothing is more fulfilling than acknowledging God. There is a difference between letting God's natural light shine in your life and walking around with a flashlight.

10

Friendship

The two best ways of being a friend are by listening and encouraging. Listen with an open heart and a closed mouth. This is not always easy, because you want to give advice, even when it is not requested. We all have situations in our lives where we know what needs to be done, but the debatable part is how and when to do it. Having a sounding board helps with the validity of your choices.

Being a good friend can be very hard when you see your friend making what you see as the wrong decision, but sometimes you have to see things through your friend's eyes. After all, it's his life. The one thing you don't want to do is help someone make the wrong decision. In the midst of her sorrow, who do you think will be blamed for the bad decision? This is a moment to pause, and the less said the better.

On the other hand, we all need encouragement from time to time. Say words that will have your friend praying and seeking God for direction in his life. Motivate her and uplift her to have the confidence to do the right thing for herself. Even if you don't agreement with him, trust your friend to live his life to the best of his ability, as you live yours.

Stand in the gap and be an intercessor for your friend. Sometimes, it's really hard to think and pray in the midst of a storm. You either pray or succumb to the storm—most people do nothing at all. If you are going to pray, don't worry; and if you are going to worry, don't pray.

Being a friend begins in your heart. There is more to being a friend than saying you are one. Friends have a special place in your life, and like everything else, they need nurturing every day.

11

Solitude

In the mist of silence came my ability to make good, sound decisions. This is where I found me. I was busy being everything to everyone in my life, and that was fine. I was at a crossroad and had to be careful of the quicksand all around me. One bad move could have me drowning. Each of us should take the time to find that special place where we can find peace—a place where the lights are dim, and the only sound is that of your heart beating. If you listen, you can hear God speaking to you, and all will be revealed to you.

I discovered that when I felt weak, I was strong beyond words.

I wrestled between fear and doubt until I found peace and a strong sense of determination. Even though my mind kept going backward, I kept my feet moving forward.

God's grace was more than enough for me. Even though I was alone, I'm never alone. I still have a lot of living, loving, sharing, and teaching to do. My life is not all about me; I had to learn to stand in the gap for others.

Living and trusting my life to God is the example I wanted to be. I wait on God, and he answers all prayers, even regarding love and companionship.

I wake up grateful each morning, so anything that happens after that is a bonus. If I wake up to a storm, God's grace and mercy will see me through.

As I wait impatiently for God to move things in my life, I know the end result always will be above and beyond anything I could have imagined.

I am learning to give my problems to God for real. The result is that I am blessed with less stress.

As my change comes in life, I am becoming a better person.

Don't apologize for being happy, blessed, and excited with life.

12

Invest in Someone's Future

I told a friend, "If you need help getting your business started, I'm here for you." My motto is "Small investment, big return."

If you need business cards or T-shirts, I'm there for you.

If you have a small restaurant, and you need someone to sit there every day and eat for free, so you look like you have customers, I'm there.

If you do hair, I will get my hair done for free and then walk around so people can ask me who did it.

If you sell designer bags, I will carry one for free, so people can see it, and I will direct them to you.

If you do makeup, I'll get made up for free, so people can see your amazing work on me.

Finally, I'll walk around in my free T-shirt, my free hairdo and makeup, carrying a free designer bag. I'll feel really good about myself, knowing how I have helped invest in someone's future.

Small investment, big return. Tell the Lord, "Thank you."

13

Embrace the New You

Don't fight the feeling. If you are happy, be happy. Live your life as a joy and not a chore. Open your heart and mind to changes. There is nothing wrong with dancing sometimes. It's good to dance to the beat of your heart. When your heart is happy, all is right with the world. You can hear that special song that touches your heart and makes you smile.

You change your hair because it makes you feel better. You decide to wear heels instead of sneakers, or stretch pants instead of jeans.

Wear makeup. Find the sexy in you, and embrace it. Be happy. Don't grow old before your time. As long as you live, there is life in you. Enjoy life's moments. There is so much more to life than watching reality shows. Be your own real-life reality. Stop watching others act out their lives on television. Learn to live yours.

Don't be afraid to ask for what you want in life Remember, you don't have to beg God for anything. He heard you the first time.

Bring back chic, dashing, and elegant.

Silence is golden in some regard. Learn to listen with your heart. Speak softly about the things you know and not what you heard. Gossiping is so unattractive. Learn to stand in the gap for others who have lost their way.

Walk in such a way that others can follow. Ladies, embrace your feminine side. The right perfume and attitude will have a man daydreaming about you. Walk in pride; speak with confidence. Men, be the leader God created you to be. God has you in the palm of his hand; act like it.

The best way to mend a broken heart or low self-esteem is piece by piece. Fake it until you make it. Before long, it will be a brand-new day.

14

Love

Everyone wants love. Love magically makes a person feel complete. True love—you never see it coming. You will be blindsided by it. One minute you're laughing and talking, and the next minute you ask yourself what in the world just happened. Don't run or try to analyze it. Embrace it as the gift it was meant to be.

People wait a lifetime for that perfect person, but there is no such thing as perfect. Perfection is only in our minds. What appears as dull and uninteresting to you may be someone's dream come true. Love operates on the inside. It's that emotion that works all by itself. The heart really wants what it wants. True love is blind because it's seen from the inside out.

When you like someone, it's from the outside in. You like the way someone looks, walks, talks, and carries himself. But you love a person's heart, her spirit, caring nature, unwavering affection, his true essence—and beauty is a bonus. Love whoever you love, and be happy.

Don't try to reconstruct a person to suit you. That's not love; that's settling. Why settle when you can wait on God. Ask God for what you want, but remember that he already knows. When you wait, it will be a match made in heaven. That's as close to perfection as you will get. When it comes to matters of the heart, we love whoever we love, sometimes without reason.

When you take the time to get to know that special someone's heart, you will find that what is missing in your own heart can be found in his or hers. This is what makes everything so complete. True love will have you daydreaming about that person and walking around with a smile on your face, because you have an amazing secret. You will feel strong and weak at the same time and wonder, "Is this for real, or am I dreaming?"

You will have butterflies just thinking of that person. Then, suddenly, you see him, and it's like no one else or nothing else matters. You are like an extension cord, and she is the plug that gives you life.

What a sense of peace in knowing you have someone to share your life with, and you don't have to pretend. That person's happiness is as important to you as yours is to him. You will have someone to laugh, smile, and talk with about anything. She loves you just as you are, even at your worst. Making each other happy and safe should be your top priority. You will have someone to dream with—and it's important to dream, because dreaming keeps hope alive.

15

Do You Choose Dreams or Love?

We all have dreams. Some dreams set the stage for our success in life. For example, you might want a job making a lot of money because you want to travel the world. How important are your dreams? Are they worth risking love for?

Sometimes you have to give up on your dreams for the sake of love. You may want to travel and do things that you feel will make your life complete. Then reality sets in, and you realize you can't afford to do all those things. You feel unfulfilled and are left with a decision. Do you continue to live for your dreams, or do you live for love?

There is a saying, "Dreams can last a lifetime." Is that true? Can you live with your dreams and be happy, or will they fade? Do you want the fairy-tale "happily ever after"? That's one thing about life—as long as you live, you have options.

16

Real Love

Real love is when …

- ➤ a man says, "The only thing I want to change about you is your name."
- ➤ you look into someone's eyes and see a rainbow.
- ➤ he is the first person you think about in the morning and the last person at night.
- ➤ the sound of her voice is the joy that gives meaning to your life.
- ➤ his smile is like an ocean breeze.
- ➤ her presence is your calm in a storm.
- ➤ you are together, and conversation is optional.
- ➤ his arms are like a coat three times too big.

➤ her ears hear your unspoken words.
➤ his legs will carry you through the quicksand of life.

But you know it's the real thing when that person likes you better than ice cream, and you like that person better than peanut butter and jelly.

17

Pause

It's okay to trip in life. Tripping is an opportunity for God to get your attention. For some of us, a small trip is all it takes to give pause in our lives. A pause gives time to think before we act. Sometimes all we really need is a pause button.

Pausing for a moment to bring clarity to your life can prevent a lot of pain and suffering.

It's much like when you were a child and had to stand in a corner. The purpose was so you would stop and think about what you had done. As adults, we don't stand in corners, even though sometimes we should. So a good trip in life serves the same purpose.

God loves us so much. He wants us to get it right the first time. And as long as we live, we are going to think the way we do things is the right way. We can't help it.

My advice is to remember that pausing is a good thing. In the middle of your crisis, pause a moment, and ask yourself, "What would Jesus do?"

Those of us who have difficulty understanding the concept of pausing need to fall down. It hurts when this happens, but it does get your attention. Sometimes, the bruises from a fall will last a lifetime. Other times, they heal gradually, and before long, you forget all about the fall and continue being the genius you think you are.

Use caution with your decision making. Learn to turn on the light when it's dark. The path has already been laid for us. All we have to do is follow God's examples in the Bible. I call it the "Book of Instructions Being Led by Examples."

We make life so much harder than it really is. Everyone wants to be the teacher, and no one wants to be the student. Life is a big school, where we learn and grow daily. There are no certificates or degrees, just one reward given by God upon completion of life.

I am learning to pause in life. I am learning to slow down, because less stress is best. I pick my battles. I choose to participate or observe certain things in life. Living can be just that simple. Pause and see.

18

Living Life as a Joy and Not a Chore

Joy comes from living life regardless of its circumstances. Learn to live in spite of setbacks or disappointments. This may not be the life you wanted, but be grateful for what you have. Without planning for tomorrow, you will continue to start over and over and never finish. Before long, life will have passed you by, and you will be stuck with the chore of carrying around regrets.

Sometimes a breakthrough is just around the corner. I have learned to be patient; after all, this is my life. The joy in life is in knowing and appreciating what's yours. Take pride in what God has trusted you with. Worrying about what others have is such a waste of living. I choose to be positive, happy, and excited with my own life.

Life's biggest disappointment may be people, if you let them. We allow them to rob us of our visions with just a few simple words. Allowing negative thoughts into our hearts tears down not only our visions but also the ability to dream.

Learn to be your own cheerleader in life and not rely on the voices of others. It's a chore to try to keep up with others. It is really hard when you feel as if you need others to validate your every move, and you try to be someone you are not. Learn to walk by faith in God.

We were all created for a purpose. Explore your heart, and find yours. Don't let your light go dim in the midst of disappointments. Change the bulb, and keep moving because victory is yours. Worry is a chore that leads to a stressful life without purpose.

I understand that my life journey is mine. If I stay focused on the things in my world and give my best, what more can I ask for? Being me is a full-time job. It requires planning, concentration, and making the best decisions for me. I wake up every day, thinking of ways to improve myself. We are all works-in-progress and should not let delays stop us from reaching our goals. If we don't find beauty in life, it will pass us by.

It's okay to sit when everyone else is standing.

Blending in is not the answer.

Focus until it becomes clear.

Wear your Sunday best every day of the week.

Laugh out loud, even if you have to cover your mouth.

If you're happy, just be happy!

Whatever you do, do it for real.

Pray about everything.

Walk victorious each day until victory is yours.

Strive each day to make God smile.

It's a chore to fight through negative thoughts daily. The joy is in knowing that nothing is too hard for God.

Don't wait for life to be perfect; get in where you fit in. Tear down invisible walls.

God truly loves you and can elevate you to places of which you can't even dream.

There is no age limit for goose pimples or butterflies.

I have learned that everything in life will not always be easy to comprehend. Any mistakes I make along the way are mine and are not made of concrete.

There are many reasons to look down, but I choose to look up in the midst of my storms. The storm may be strong, and the pressure of fighting the wind might be unbearable, but the end is always worth fighting for.

Every one of us faces obstacles. Regardless to who you are, obstacles can keep you from reaching your personal goals in life and from feeling complete. Obstacles may keep you from feeling you are the very best that you can be. Sometimes the more you have, the greater the obstacle.

I know that life's everyday challenges can be difficult, but I also know that I am surrounded by God's favor and that each step I take is no surprise to him. He will allow me to go to the left sometimes and then to the right, until I realize he always has been right in front of me, leading me all the way.

People can be your biggest obstacle, either at your job or in a social setting. We give people far more power over us than we should. In the workplace, there is a chain of command. In order to keep your job, you have to abide by rules and regulation. We should remember, however, who really is in charge. When people come against you in a negative way, God can turn it around. Make your enemies your stepping stones to success.

When we give your life to God, nothing is too hard to conquer. God can change your situation in seconds, and what began as a battle becomes a victory.

I know that if I live right, treat people right, and keep God first, nothing can stop me from my destiny.

19

Second Chance

Don't miss your second chance in life, because when it comes, it's most often unexpected. Prepare yourself for the unknown, and embrace any and all changes that come your way.

I personally grew very weary of waiting for my second chance. My days turned to weeks, and weeks turned to months, and then months to years. I had no choice but to wait on God, and waiting is something I am not good at. Nothing was happening, and nothing changed. But I kept praying, because that was something I could do. It was possible for me to ask God to help me, to give me strength and patience, and he did.

But it took time—a lot of sleepless nights and stressful days; a lot of wondering just what the future had in store for me. As time went by, a feeling of calm came over me. I could finally rest, knowing it was out of my hands. Then, suddenly, one day I felt a very soft breeze. This breeze was the pages of my life turning ever so smoothly. There was a moment of reconnecting. During this process I had to remember the past and embrace my future.

Before me now were new opportunities, hopes, dreams, and desire. I had an opportunity to accomplish more this time around and be the best me I could be. This was my "woulda, coulda, shoulda" moment in life.

Take advantage of it when it comes for you. I am prepared to take boldness to a new level. Even though my heart was broken at one time, it began to feel whole again. I could look someone straight in the eye and feel joy again. I could actually hear the humor in someone's voice, and before long, I was laughing again. I could feel someone's touch and feel safe again.

I am learning that I cannot expect people to make me happy. My joy and happiness comes from God—and that's guaranteed.

Enjoy God's beauty. Every day is a good day if you have faith and if you believe. The knowledge you have obtained over the years and the knowledge yet to be learned will make you a force to be reckoned with. Tell others of the goodness of God on a daily bases. He is good all the time.

I tell God every day, "It's me and you against the world." What an adventure my life has become. Each day is filled with growth and excitement. And I take nothing for granted.

As with anything new, fear will come. But I don't let it stop me from moving forward in life. Wear fear as a shoelace on your sneakers as you walk through life. Walk from what was to what will be.

I was introduced to God at an early age. My sitter was a sanctified older lady who had prayer meetings at her house during the week. The women at the meetings wore long, starched white dresses and used washboards for the music.

My brother, who was three years older, and I were told to get on our knees and call on Jesus. Sometimes I fell asleep but not for long, because the shouting would wake me up. I would look at my brother and say, "When does Mama come home? I'm tired of calling Jesus."

Then, as I got older, my dad would always say to me, "Fear of the Lord is the beginning of wisdom." I had no idea what that meant, but I knew if my dad said it, then it was very important and very true. I went to Vacation Bible School during the summers, and one year I learned a phrase that has been my favorite for years:

"Therefore, my beloved brethren, be steadfast, immovable, always abounding **in** the work of the Lord, knowing that your labor is not in vain in the Lord" (1 Corinthians 15:58).

This was a song, and I sung in the choir. I couldn't wait for the Sundays when we would sing it. Again, I had no idea what it meant back then, but I heard what it said and knew it was very important and very true. God's Word can enter your heart at a young age and be with you always. Even now, I may not understand every word in the Bible, but I hear what it says.

Wisdom has taught me to seek understanding. I now know

my favorite phrase tells me that if I stand on God's Word, no matter what life brings my way, all things are possible.

I know that we, as people, are composed of layers. What you see is not always the true person. We are born with a soft layer of skin, and as we grow, the skin gets thicker and thicker. Each layer represents a trial or lesson learned in life. That's why in order to help others, it's important to be patient and peel back each layer until you reach their hearts. Sometimes, even after reaching the heart, you will need to find a way to get in it. Don't be so quick to give up on people. Remember that one day a life saved was yours.

20

Being Different

It's okay to be different. To think and feel the way you do is what makes you unique. Sometimes you miss your blessing in trying to be like others. I learned years ago that being me was okay. There is not another person on earth like me. I don't need others to validate who I am.

Just because someone looks at you funny does not mean there is anything wrong with you. I expect people to stare at me. When I walk in a room, smile, or speak, it's the God in me they see. Who wouldn't stare at that? Being with a group of people all the time means you are one in a crowd. Learn to be by yourself, and discover you. You will be amazed what you learn about yourself and what you have to offer.

Also, it's okay to say no. I say no on a daily basis. I practice saying no, so that when the time comes, I'm ready. Using a smile when you say no is optional. I was called a rebel once by someone because I said no. It was not meant as a compliment. It meant I didn't follow the crowd. I stood on my beliefs and found myself alone. It didn't feel good at the time, but I held on to my belief. In the end, I felt good, knowing I could think and make decisions for myself. When you realize all you need is God, nothing else matters.

There are all kinds of people in the world. A person who is shy is drawn to someone talkative. Someone who has never traveled is fascinated by someone who has stories of travel to tell. A large person may be drawn to a small person because it gives him a feeling of power and strength, while a small person is drawn to a large person for comfort and safety. It's like a circle broken in half. They are the same but different because one faces one way, and the other faces another way. But together, they make a whole. I like being different. It shows strength, builds character, and pushes me to my limit.

This is where greatness comes from. It will keep you wanting to strive for more. So test the waters of life, and don't limit your blessings.

21

Foundation

Following the path already placed for us is easy. All the hard work and sacrifices, along with praying for grace and mercy, has already been made. We all have generations of prayers stored up on our behalf that we should be thankful for. We are not worthy of God's goodness or his love, but because our parents, grandparents, and great-grandparents knew that the only way to make it in life was with God, here we are today. Remember your life is not all yours. The decisions you make today affect others. Begin now to store your house with praises and blessings for your future generations. It's not too late for you to build that yellow brick road for others to follow.

We have lost sight along the way of what is really important in life and how valuable life is. Men must learn to be leaders and not followers. Just think of the power you have when you speak—the knowledge and skills you are capable of sharing, the love and compassion you carry around in your hearts for others. We are a proud people with a strong heritage. Let's not let the Devil tear us down because of hopelessness, helplessness, and lack of vision. The difference between right and wrong was instilled in us at an early age. It's just waiting to be taught as a blueprint for living.

What's on the outside does not reflect what's inside a person's heart. I am excited for that moment when young men truly realize their worth and show the dignity that goes with being a man. Find your invisible cape that's blowing nonstop, waiting for you to take control of it and be the best that you can be. There was a time when pride and a man's word was all a man had. He would work all day for his family for a few dollars. But the sense of pride in knowing he was providing for his family went a long way. A real man takes care of his own and sets examples for others. We all knew when Daddy came home that everything would be okay.

Live responsibly and carry yourself is such a way that others will see hope through you. Set godly examples for our youth. It's never too late.

I am excited about life and blessed to have a second chance. I strive to live with as few regrets as I can. I want to have as little stress as possible. I choose to let my past be a stepping stone for my tomorrow. I will step fearlessly toward life's possibilities. I will learn to say yes and boldly ponder my new horizon. I will wear my cape at all times, knowing the way has already been made for me, and there is nothing in my past or future too hard to conquer. That the same God who was with me yesterday will be with me always. As long as I know the truth, I have direction.

It's okay to reflect, but I don't let it dictate to me. In all phases of my life, I will keep moving forward. God has such wonderful plans for me—for each of us. I get up each morning and thank God for another opportunity to get my life right— and God says, "I'll take it from here. Follow me." I started smiling, and before long, I was laughing.

Don't give up. Keep living.

22

Suddenly

Windows and doors are opened, and I am basking in the blessings of life.

I was caught completely off guard. I was unprepared. My fresh, just-mended heart is bursting again but this time for a different reason. Life, with its hopes, dreams, and possibilities, are played before me. I have new meaning in my life.

As I boldly go where I have never been before, it's with an open mind. As I shed my fears and fasten my cape, I am ready to soar to new heights each day. I'm excited about what God has in store for me. I believe that every setback is a setup for a comeback. Thank God for the comeback. I will take my comeback and walk in victory. I am the producer, and God is the director of my life. I work hard to stay on the yellow brick road placed before me. I strive to add new bricks along the way.

It's not the number of bricks I lay that matters but the quality and the foundation.

Don't give up on life because of what you see. Live your life because of what you know to be true. I wake up every morning, thankful for another opportunity to just live. I don't take waking up for granted. If you were not happy with yesterday, take this opportunity to write a better day today. Don't carry negative thoughts around with you. Think positive, and receive what's already yours.

When you know the voice of God and seek him daily for direction in your life, you will have finally arrived. You will have reached that place where the true meaning of life is revealed. It's when we realize it's not about me or you. It's never been about us. It's about what we can do for others.

"God so loved us that he gave his only son." Once we master the true meaning of love and giving, God's blessings will overtake us. We are servants to each other. We are always seeking to receive instead of give. I have found the one thing I am best at is giving of myself. My time, a kind word, a smile, a prayer, encouragement—there is no price on kindness. Believe me when I tell you that kindness goes a long way. And it is not easily forgotten. Each of us, whether we are giving or receiving, will go from hopeless to overcome, from doubtful to trustful, and from being a victim to being victorious. I would say that is a life worth living.

23

Nuggets for Life

- ➢ Learn to live in the moment.
- ➢ Accept people just the way they are, without unattainable expectations.
- ➢ Open your heart to love without any restrictions.
- ➢ Don't be afraid to get your blessing. If you asked without reservations, receive it with boldness.
- ➢ Don't be afraid to ask for what you want. Then receive it with a grateful heart.
- ➢ Love with all your heart.
- ➢ Renew your mind and body daily.
- ➢ Being safe feels comfortable, but dare to reach for higher goals in life. Put yourself to the test.
- ➢ Don't wait for a tsunami to come into your life to get on your knees.

> Carry your first-aid kit with you every day, filled with compassion, encouragement, kindness, patience, and understanding.

> Life's journey consists of traveling down winding roads of uncertainty, passing uninhabited spaces, crossing oceans of unlimited water, and riding immeasurable waves. But through it all, we still reach our destinations and purposes.

> Being grateful should be a way of life.

> Help others with no hidden agenda.

> Smile, because it not only looks good but feels good.

> Walking and talking like a Christian is contagious.

> Wisdom is meant to be shared.

> Youth and old age are phases; treat them as phases.

> True love will have you rushing through your day just so you can sit down and think about it.

> The future can be scary if you are unprepared for it.

> Being a parent is more than giving life. It's being a coach for life.

> If you walk ahead of me, I can't hear you. If you walk behind me, I can't see you. Let's walk hand in hand and explore the world together.

> Say what you feel.

> Fix whatever is broken.

> Look at love, and feel love looking back.

24

Finally

As I start this new chapter in my life, the possibilities are endless. As I run my race, no matter what goes on around me, I will stay focused. I won't be afraid of anything new. New is truly exciting.

We are not always prepared for life, but we should prepare to live it, regardless. My new motto in life is "To my own self be true." The answer to any question that starts with "can you," "could you," or "would you" is no! Not unless it is an extreme emergency.

If you are fortunate to have someone to travel on life's journey with you, realize it is a blessing.

I am thankful for new opportunities. What an incredible year this has been for me. God has blessed me beyond my dreams. Each day is a visual reminder that nothing is too hard for him and that he truly answers prayer.

We ask for what we want, and God always gives us what we need. I pinch myself sometimes, just to make sure I'm not dreaming. I look in the mirror and see a smile so big that all I can say is, "Jesus loves me; this I know." I have also been blessed with the most handsome grandson in the world. My life is truly amazing.

My highs are higher. My smiles are brighter, and my dreams are visible. The air feels fresh and clean, and my heart is beating to a brand new beat. Each day is filled with great expectations, and it's only today. *Wait until tomorrow!*

Printed in the United States
By Bookmasters